From Addiction

to Recovery

Lady K.

ISBN 978-1-64468-903-5 (Paperback)
ISBN 978-1-64468-904-2 (Digital)

Covenant Books, Inc.
11661 Hwy 707
Murrells Inlet, SC 29576
www.covenantbooks.com

— *Dedication Page* —

— *Testimonial* —

This book is the beginning of a beautiful journey to a life full of faith, strength, love, determination, perseverance, and most of all, courage. It is a reminder for the readers to continue to remember to live and follow the Word of our Lord Jesus Christ, not only through our toughest moments, but in every aspect of our lives. It is a true testament and reflection of the person writing this book, my friend, Kathleen Hall, who inspires me every day to live a meaningful and fulfilling life.

—Marisol Lopez, Entrepreneur, Wife, and Mother

— Contents —

— 1 —

No More Anxiety

Your heart is beating so fast. Why do you think you have heart palpitations?

Here's a list of symptoms:

- Skipping heartbeats
- Racing heartbeat
- Hard pounding of the heart
- Pain
- Pressure
- Tightness of the chest

Let us write down your causes:

Now, when you write down these causes, you will feel a release. You will begin a new you. God, I pray in the name of Jesus that You begin a new work in this person. Only you can heal. Now Father, I know You are a healer because You heal me from any stress. Let's begin to give thanks to God for your healing. Take as much time as you may need and return to this book.

Write down how you feel:

The Bible says, "Ask and it will be given to you; seek and you will find; knock and the door will be opened to you" (Matthew 7:7).

—— 2 ——

Sadness

Why are you sad?

Write it down:

Do you feel hurt? The reason you feel this way is because a long time ago, someone hurt you as a child. They took away your childhood innocence.

I want you to forgive this person right now. Don't do it for them, but do it for you. I know this will hurt at first, but do it now. I am here with you. I feel your pain. Now tell yourself that the hurt will now end, and as you shed your tears, forgive the person or the people who have hurt you. It will hurt, but only then can you begin to heal.

Let's write:

No more sadness. Let's begin a new life. Let's ask God for forgiveness for the wasted years and for the years of hurt. From this day forward, no more seconds will be wasted.

The Bible says, "Trust in the lord with all your heart, and do not lean on your own understanding. In all your ways acknowledge Him, and He will make straight your paths" (Proverbs 3:5–6).

— 3 —

Stinking and Thinking

We sit and think about why our thoughts are distorted. We sit and think about the past. But why?

Write down why:

Think about where this bad sinking and thinking comes from. Let us go back to the past as far back as you can remember.

This will be a healing moment for you. You have to go back so that you can clear the memory from your mind.

I am here with you as you write down your past thoughts:

When this is all over, you will feel so much better. You will be healed at this moment. I can feel your pain fading away.

The Bible says, "O Lord, if you heal me, I will be truly healed; if you save me, I will be truly saved. My praises are for you alone" (Jeremiah 17:14 NLT).

—— 4 ——

Addiction

There are different kinds of addiction, such as:

1. Sex/Lust
2. Porn
3. Overeating
4. Anger
5. Depression
6. Technology/Internet
7. Drugs
8. Shopping
9. Control
10. Rage
11. Envy
12. Favoritism

These are only a few addictions. There are many more that exist that you should be wary of.

5

Anger

Anger leads to sin. The Bible says, "The acts of sinful nature are obvious: sexual immorality, impurity, and debauchery; idolatry and witchcraft; hatred, discord, jealousy, fits of rage, selfish ambition, dissentions, factions, and envy; drunkenness, orgies, and the like. I warn you, as I did before, that those who live like this will not inherit the kingdom of God" (Galatians 5:19–21).

Therefore, the definition of anger is to have a strong feeling of annoyance, displeasure, or hostility. This is why we need to pray for patience. Anger needs to be removed from our minds. How? I am glad you asked.

The Bible says, "Get rid of all bitterness, rage, and anger; brawling and slander, along with every form of malice. Be kind and compassionate to one another, forgiving each other, just as Christ God forgave you" (Ephesians 4:31–32).

—— 6 ——

Depression

Depression is of the devil. The definition of depression is to feel severe despondency and dejection accompanied by inadequacy. Why do I say this? Anything that works against God's will is the work of the Devil. David confessed his sin.

The Bible says, "Have mercy on me, O' God, according to your unfailing love; according to your great compassion, blot out my transgressions. Wash away my iniquity and cleanse me from my sin. For I know my transgressions, and my sin is always before me. Against you, you only, have I sinned and done what is evil in your sight, so that you are proved right when you speak and justified when you judge. Surely, I was sinful at birth, sinful from the inner, the time my mother conceived me. Surely you desire truth in the inner parts; you teach me wisdom in the inmost place. Cleanse me with hyssop, and I will be clean; wash me and I will be whiter than snow" (Psalms 51:1–7).

— 7 —

Alcohol

Alcohol is the Devil's way of luring you away from God. What does it mean to be an alcoholic? Excessively drinking or using alcohol to bring people to their lowest state; at this point, your body is not yours to abuse.

The Bible says, "[D]o you not know that your body is the temple of the Holy Ghost who is in you, whom you have from God, and you are not your own" (1 Corinthians 6:19).

Just imagine this: When you lay with someone, Jesus is with you. Wise people say that a mind is a terrible thing to waste. Being drunk does not excuse you from being a child of God.

The Bible says, "Woe to him who gives drink to his neighbors, pouring it from the wineskin till they are drunk, so that he can gaze on their naked bodies. You will be filled with shame instead of glory. Now, it is your turn! Drink and be exposed! The cup from the LORD'S right hand is coining around to you, and disgrace will cover your glory" (Habakkuk 2:15–16).

—— 8 ——

Emotional Pain/Hurt

Feeling emotion means to suffer mentally or emotionally, distress. How do we understand emotion? How can we identify it and release it? We have released emotion through many ways, such as anxiety, anger, control, sadness, depression, inadequacy, confusion, hurt, loneliness, guilt, and shame. Notice how most of these emotions are based on fear.

The Bible says, "Do not let your hearts be troubled. Trust in God; trust also in me," (John 14:1).

I am familiar with this addiction all too well. I have been hurt by the people closest to me; my partner, for example. I was sleeping with the enemy. It was a very frightening experience for me. This person was supposed to have the love of God, but he talked about me behind my back to my own family. This hurt me so bad. Not to mention, he was a liar and a thief. He was caught with an item that should not have been in his bags.

Pray to Jesus that He will work this out for you. He worked it out for me. Amen.

—— 9 ——

Deception

Satan is the one who leads us all astray. What does deception even mean? It means the state of being deceived. The Bible says, "[h]e is the father of lies," (John 8:44).

We as Christians are so blind when it comes to Satan's tricks. We are deceived because Satan makes everything look good but never shows us the negative consequences to our actions. By the time you realize that you have been tricked, it is too late to do anything about it. The Devil deliberately blinds the eyes of the people so that they cannot see the glory of God in the face of Jesus Christ.

The Bible says, "I beseech you, therefore brethren, by the mercies of God, that you present your bodies a living sacrifice, holy, acceptable to God, which is your reasonable service. And do not be conformed to this world but be ye transformed by the renewing of your mind, that you may prove what is good and acceptable and the perfect will of God" (Romans 12:1–2).

— 10 —

Overcoming Deceit

What does it mean to deceive someone? When you deceive, you conceal or misrepresent the truth.

There is a story in the Bible surrounding Judah and Tamar. You see, Tamar wanted a child so bad that she disguised herself as a prostitute. During this time, prostitutes concealed their faces, and she was without child due to her father-in-law having lied to her about promising her his youngest son. He did not hold up his promise, so Tamar lost faith and became a prostitute to have sex with Judah in order to conceive.

Does this remind you of a situation in your life or in someone else's life? Deceit can be very hurting to a person and to you as well. We need to be true to ourselves.

The Bible says, "Judah recognized them immediately and said, 'She is more righteous than I am, because I didn't arrange for her to marry my son Shelah'… And Judah never slept with Tamar again". Deceit may be everywhere, but with God by our side, we can overcome it.

— 11 —
Hatred/Envy

What is hatred? Hatred is an intense hostility and aversion usually stemming from fear, anger, or sense of injury. What is envy? Envy is a feeling of discontent or resentful longing created by someone else's possessions, qualities, or luck.

There is a story in the Bible where two brothers give offerings to God; one is good, and the other offering is bad. Anger settled into one of the brothers, the one that God was unhappy with, so this brother began to hate his brother.

The Bible says, "A fool gives full vent to his anger, but a wise man keeps himself under control" (Proverbs 29:11).

One brother felt competitive with the other because God accepted one offering but not the other offering. So the brother decided to take matters into his own hands. The envious brother deceived his brother to go out into the fields to hunt. While hunting, the envious brother decided to attack and kill the brother that had God's favor (Genesis 4:1–8). God expects us to give Him our best gifts since He gave us His best gift in the form of His only Son, Jesus Christ.

— 12 —

Abuse

What is abuse, you ask? Rape. Sexual Assault. Sexual Molestation. Can anyone tell me why we abuse one another? A mind is a terrible thing to lay to waste. How can someone stoop so low as to hurt an innocent child? Our minds are capable of corruption. Sexual temptation is hard to resist, even if we are made aware of the dangers and consequences of having promiscuous sex. If sex is among our addictions, we must run from any and all situations where we might fall prey to sin.

As the Bible reminds us, "Lust is a sin, desire that begins in the mind... But I tell you that anyone who looks at a woman lustfully has already committed adultery with her in his heart" (Matthews 5:28).

Do you know what bothers me most? The fact that Christians are the ones molesting the innocent! Lust is called on by the lack of obedience to God's Word.

The Bible tells us, "[B]ut the worries of this life, the deceitfulness of wealth and the desires for other things come in and choke the word, making it unfruitful..." (Mark 4:19).

— 13 —

Recurrent Addiction: Sin

To sin is to commit an immoral act considered to be a transgression against divine law.

Why can't we seem to shake this problem off? We may feel awkward about bringing our recurrent sin before God. Dealing with the same issues time and time again is preferable to admitting them out loud. What are we supposed to do with this addiction? This question has taken over my life completely. Confess your addiction to God and really mean it. We must recognize our flaws. John says that God will forgive us and cleanse us from every wrong.

Recovery is a process that takes time to reach its full cycle. There is a strong contrast between the light in the Christian way of life and the darkness in the life led by sin. Most of the time, we claim to be Christian, but our lives are cover in darkness. We lie to ourselves about how much control we give up to sin. Light and darkness cannot coexist in our hearts. One will always prevail above the other.

The Bible tells us, "This message we heard from Jesus and now declare to you: God is light, and there is no darkness in him at all. So we are lying if we say we have fellowship with God, but go on living in spiritual darkness; we are not" (1 John 1:5–6).

— 14 —

Conformity

Conformity means to adhere to the pressures of following a fixed standard, regulation, or social acceptability. People seem to allow their thoughts to be controlled by people of the world, conforming to the world, following the world—a vicious cycle, so to speak.

The Bible reminds us of this, "[A]nd so, dear brothers and sisters. I plead with you to give your body to God because of all He has done for you. Let them be living and holy sacrifice, the kind He will find acceptable. This is truly the way to worship him. Do not copy the behavior and custom of the world, but let God transform you into a new person by changing the way you think. Then, you will learn to know God's will for you, which is good and pleasing and perfect" (Roman 12:1–2).

Once we get it in our minds, reading the scripture is the only way for us to really change. It is not our will for us to change but God's will. Peter believes we are like newborn babies, and a believer's growth in holiness is like "growing up in salvation."

Why is it that Peter, James, John, and Jesus have to constantly remind us Christians about our behavior?

Many have struggled with the temptation of escaping the painful realities by turning to the pleasures of this world. These worldly pleasures feel so good to the soul, but that could not be further from the truth.

— 15 —

Adultery

Adultery. I think we have all heard of this at some point in our lives whether through movies, television shows, or real-life experience; but for those of us who have not been exposed to the idea yet, it means to be sexually involved with someone outside the bonds of marriage.

Loving someone outside of marriage is a sin. God gave us love to keep in secret with our spouse. Is it really hard to make love to just one person? No, not if your heart is right with God.

We know that temptation will come. This is why you need to be strong. Pray and ask God to help you in this area of your life. Do not watch a movie, look at porn, binge watch television shows, or sit around being lazy. The Bible constantly reinforces that having an idle mind leaves you ripe for participating in sin. When we sit around and do nothing, sin is the only thing that keeps the mind occupied.

You must not take what belongs to another person; in this case, a mate. "You shall not steal…" (Exodus 20:15). God commands us all: No adultery. It is His law.

— 16 —

Unholy Living

The Bible calls upon us to have self-control. We all seem to allow our flesh to control every aspect of our lives.

Let me be real for a second. Why do we as Christians allow the Devil to have control over us? We will always be tempted if we do not change how we think.

The Bible dictates, "[W]e have a priceless inheritance—inheritance that is kept in Heaven for you, pure and undefiled, beyond the reach of change and decay. And through your faith, God is protecting you by his power until you receive this salvation, which is ready to be revealed on the last day for all to see" (1 Peter 1:4–5).

In our most critical state, we fail to see God in our state of mind. We have to learn that He is with us in every problem, in every situation. He said even if you make your bed in hell, He will be with you.

Somebody says recovery. You are recovering right now "in the name of Jesus."

Allow God to help you to strengthen you in your recovery now. We will continue to struggle in our mortal bodies. "Let go and let God in."

— 17 —

Favoritism/Prejudice

What does it mean to practice favoritism? It means you give unfair treatment to one person or group at the expense of another person or group.

Why do we even feel prejudice toward each other? It may be because that other person might not have what you have, so you do not hang around with them. They seem to be less than you are. The people you surround yourself with share similar tastes or values.

The Bible reminds us not to judge one another. Is this a sin? The Bible says, "My dear brothers and sisters, how can you claim to have faith in our glorious Lord Jesus Christ if you favor some people over others" (James 2:1–4)?

For example, suppose you come to a meeting dressed in fancy clothes and expensive jewelry, and another person comes in dressed in worn and dirty clothing. If your boss gives you special attention and a good seat but tells the other person to stand off to the side or to sit on the floor, doesn't this prove that your boss's judgments are guided by evil motions?

Therefore, it is so important for you not to think highly of yourselves as the Bible tells us, "If you favor someone, you are committing a sin. You are guilty of breaking the law."

— 18 —

Resentment

To feel resentment is to feel anger due to real or imagined injury/offense.

What causes resentment? Why do you feel this? Most of the time, it comes from family resenting one another. We see people we know, say things about them, then we begin not to like them. Why is this?

We imitate what we see. Let me give you some reasons why. She might be prettier than you; her hair might be long; they have more money, etc. You get the point. Can I be honest?

The Bible warns us about these things: "If you keep on biting and devouring each other, watch out or you will be destroyed by each other" (Galatians 5:15).

With resentment, we tear each other down with words. We claim that words do not hurt. I bet you that you know of someone who has died from talking too much. It is a shame how we do this to one another. If only you could understand how you have hurt the person you hate or resent; it is not nice to feel this way. I am sure you know the feeling. Why are we still with people that hurt us?

Leave them; start a new life. If they do not want to change, then you can change. Move on, forgive, and forget them.

— 19 —

Kill

What does it mean to kill? To kill is to cause the death of a person, animal, or thing. Murder, on the other hand, is the unlawful premeditated killing of one human by another.

The person that I speak of is a person that persecuted the church. You may know of someone that is like this man. Maybe they did not physically kill, but they have killed the church and God's people through words.

The Bible says, "Those who are dominated by the sinful nature think about sinful things, but those who are controlled by the Holy Spirit think about things that please the Spirit… That's why those who are still under the control of their sinful nature can never please God" (Romans 8:5–8).

It just amazes me how we as Christians think that we can outsmart God. There is no way that can be. It is imperative to admit your addiction and acknowledge its destructiveness, for "nothing is impossible with God" (Luke 1:37).

The man that I speak of was called out by name by God: "Saul, Saul! Why are you persecuting me?"

What I appreciate most about Paul was that he was very obedient to God's Word. If he can change, so can you. Saul's name was later changed to Paul.

You might be a killer in the Church: A Spirit-killer.

— 20 —

Dysfunction

Dysfunction: abnormal functioning. Why do we play around with the problems we have in our families? We are told what to do in this family and to stay in this family, and you wonder why Mary is so crazy...

People get help. It's okay for you to get help. When I say get help, I do not mean the crazy kind of help but the therapeutic kind; the kind of help that is provided when you just go and talk to someone. When we do talk to someone, it is just for money. Why? Is it because we are too lazy to work? Can I be real here?

We all have abnormal situations in our family. Seek help. I know someone who can help you for sure. His name is Jesus. He is the only one who can set you free from your dysfunctional problems.

We all need recovery so bad. The church is not talking about this anymore, I know. Therefore, I am here to help you. I love and care for you and I do not know you. Why, you ask? It is because I have Jesus in my life. You can also have Him in yours. All you have to do is call on the name of Jesus Christ, and He will take care of all of your needs.

The Bible says, "If you confess with your mouth that Jesus is Lord and believe in your heart that God was raised from the dead, you will all be saved" (Romans 10:9).

From Addiction to Recovery

— Part Two —

Love God First!

How can I love someone I cannot see?

Loving God whom you can see is easy when you go through some pain, hurt, avoid, emptiness, lonely feelings. Who do you pray to? Is there someone you talk to?

What professing Christian would ever say that God is not first in their life? But what does your mind saying? Will you not say that God is not first? But how are you living? What is your life saying?

The Bible says in Matthew 15:8, "These people honor me with their lips, but their hearts are far from me."

Why do we say we love God, but as soon as something happen, we then call on the name of the Lord? But God is not first.

Jacob died, but God lives on. As we read further in the book of Genesis, we see that the God of Abraham, Isaac, and Jacob became the God of Joseph also.

Remember the life of Joseph? Hated by his own brothers, he was thrown in a pit, sold as a slave to Potiphar in Egypt, thrown into prison, and forgotten. But throughout all Joseph's life, God was with Joseph and made him whole. God was with Joseph in all that he went through in Potiphar's house and in the prison. God exalted Joseph and made him the King of Egypt.

Look at your life now. God had your back at all times.

When you serve the true and living, you come out on top. Amen.

What Is Your Calling for Your Life?

When do we question those who do not seek God? Who and what should one marry? What career do I pursue in school? What job should I take? Shall I live home or leave? And of course, what is my ministry?

1. Pray
2. Seek
3. Call on the Lord
4. Fast
5. Write

The Bible says, "Then the LORD replied: 'Write down the revelation and make it plain on tablets so that a herald may run with it'" (Habakkuk 2:2).

What do you think the Lord means by "write down and make it plain?"

I pray that God will use you in a mighty way.

Living in God's Purpose

The Bible says, "Let there be real harmony among you so there won't be any spirit in the church. I pled with you to be of one mind, united in thoughts and purpose (1 Corinthians 1:10).

Living in Gods purpose means you will honor and obey his law of guidance. This is important to obey the Word of the Lord, the Bible. To obey is better than sacrifice.

Rules:

1. Obey
2. Honor
3. Sacrifice
4. Listen
5. Study

The Bible clearly states that God created man and women; He created him for His glory. Therefore, the ultimate purpose of man, according to the Bible, is simply to glorify God.

We can worship God with all our hearts. Call on the name of the Lord not when you are in need but now when everything is going right. Amen.

God loves you so much, He gave His only son… (Fill in the rest of the scripture)

As Far Back as You Can Remember, Think Back

It's okay to think back. You will begin to have a breakthrough.

Have you ever wondered why you act the way you do?

You are not mentally ill. This is something you have seen and experienced. This is a real private moment for you, so be still and listen to the voice of God.

The Bible says: "To hear God's voice, we must belong to God." Jesus said, "My sheep listen to my voice; I know them, and they follow me" (John 10:27).

These are some reasons:

1. Both Dad and Mom
2. DNA
3. Grandparents

Everything you experience is learned behavior.

Let's begin to speak life into your situation. Hurt, in the name of Jesus, be gone. I pray in the name of Jesus that God will touch and heal in the name of Jesus, I speak life over my situation now; my life is changed now and forever. Amen.

Now write down and speak life.

Unleashing the Anger Inside of You

Definition of unleash: to free from or as if from a leash; let loose; unleashing his or her anger.

Definition of potential: Having or showing the capacity to become or develop into something in the future.

Anger leaves you feeling torn up inside. Head is pounding ninety, going north. Your face is ugly. And your muscles are so tight. Every inch of your body is racking with pain. You cannot eat or sleep or function like a human being.

Unleash the screaming monster that rages inside you. You will lose control, lash out, and retaliate.

Before this happens, let us write what is make you angry.

Addictive Forms of Anger

A need in having what you can not have is where the anger become expressive. This behavior is a learned behavior, seen by other that are around you, the act of this condition.

Addictive, I need. Addiction can be any form of condition that will take the place of habit form, such as alcohol, drug, sex, porn and this is the works of the devil.

Definition of addictive: the fact or condition of being addicted to a particular substance, thing, or activity.

Definition of Aggressive:

Definition of Depressive:

The Bible says, "But the fruit of the Spirit is love, joy, peace, longsuffering, gentleness, goodness, faith, Meekness, temperance: against such there is no law" (Galatians 5:22–23 KJV).

Make a list.

Disarmed

Post-traumatic Stress Disorder develops in the form of learning. This disease is learned by seeing, hearing, and experiences.

We will learn how to disarm disease called PTSD today in the name of Jesus. This is because no name or weapon is formed against you that shall prosper, in the name of Jesus. Call those things out as though they were.

> "No weapon formed against you shall prosper, and every tongue *which* rises against you in judgment You shall condemn. This is the heritage of the servants of the LORD, and their righteousness is from Me," says the LORD. (Isaiah 54:17)

A list of disorders:

1. Anxiety
2. Fear/anger
3. Reckless behavior
4. Sleep disturbance
5. Aggressive
6. Hypervigilance

From one to six, write down a list of the opposite.

Integrating the Two of You

The split self is the other person inside of you that acts out. He or she can be a real mess. Let me begin to tell you where they come from. They come from little you, from a child. The person that I speak of is the little person that lives inside of you from your childhood.

1. She is called bipolar.
2. Family gives it a name.
3. Mentally ill.
4. Crazy.

This person is real. She or he has become split way back when. Why? This little me is the one that was hurt—hit, beaten, raped, abused, bullied, and much more.

This little person is the one that comes out of you as a grown person, and you do not know where the little person come from.

1. Little person
2. Brittleness
3. Drugs
4. Alcohol

Please write as far back as you can remember.

Interpersonal Skills

A. Confidence

It is important to have confidence of your interactions with people; to ensure others to believe in your words and actions, trustworthiness in family, friends, and coworkers; to demonstrate you've been listening to others and with respect of their opinion.

Definition of confidence: The feeling or belief that one can rely on someone or something; firm trust.

B. Empathy

When you disagree with someone, family, friends, and coworkers, it's important to understand their point of view. For example, "I understand where you are coming from." This means that you have been listening and you respect their opinions.

Definition of empathy: The ability to understand and share the feelings of another.

C. Open-Minded

A communicator enters a conversation with flexibility, open to listen, and understands the person's point of view simply because of understanding the person's views.

Definition of open-minded: Willing to consider new ideas; unprejudiced.

Write down some ways to improve.

Reshaping Your Relation with Self

Emotional intelligence is the ability to identify, understand, use, and manage one's own emotions in positive ways to relieve stress, communicate effectively, empathize with others, overcome hurt, and avoid conflict.

1. Develop self-awareness.
2. Manage emotions.
3. Communicate with self-talk.

Can we really come to some kind of reasoning with ourselves?

To recognize who we really are in self, to begin to be real with self to bring out the true you; have you ever noticed how other people talk to you very disrespectfully? Why is that? Take back your power.

1. How do you feel about yourself?
2. Be committed to you.
3. Ask for help.

The Bible says, "You will make known to me the path of life: In Your presence is fullness of joy; In Your right hand there are pleasures forever" (Psalm 16:11).

Take notes:

Sadness

Why are you sad?

Write it down.

Do you feel hurt? The reason you feel this way is because a long time ago, someone hurt you as a child and took away your childhood.

I want you to forgive this person right now. Do it for yourself first. I know this hurts. Do it now. I am here with you. I feel your hurt. Now tell yourself, "I have spent all my life hurting, but today it ends right now." As you begin to cry, forgive the person or persons that hurt you. I know it hurts. Do it now.

Let's write:

No more sadness.
Let's begin a new life.
Let's ask God for forgiveness for wasted years and years of hurt from this day forward, no more wasted seconds.

The Bible says, "Trust in the LORD with all your heart, and do not lean on your own understanding. In all your ways acknowledge him, and he will make straight your paths" (Proverbs 3:5–6).

Nonverbal Communication Skills

1. Clarity and Concision

Try to message as few words as possible. Be direct and clear when you're speaking or not; face-to-face is better than via e-mail or phone.

Rambling is not a good sign. The listener will tune you out, "What is this person trying to say?" you will be able to encourage the person to engage in more honest communication.

Write down your skills.

Definition of clarity: The quality of being clear, in particular. Or the quality of coherence and intelligibility.

Definition of concision: The quality or state of being concise or archaic: a cutting up or off.

Now let's begin with learning to have clarity.

Just as I stated before, to learn these skills will take some time to form habits. Take time to think something before you speak. This will help you to avoid confessing to your audience or avoid excessive talking, loss of words with no understanding.

Nonverbal Communication

Body language, hand gestures, eye contact. Nonverbal communication includes facial expressions, a tone and voice, gestures displayed through body language *(kinesics)*, the physical between the communicators *(proxemics)*.

Definition of Kinesics: The study of the way in which certain body movements and gestures serve as a form of nonverbal communication.

Definition of Proxemics: The branch of knowledge that deals with the amount of space that people feel it necessary to set between themselves and others.

For example, people nod their heads vigorously, saying, "Yes" to emphasize they agree with the other person but shrugging the shoulders is a sad expression, saying, "I'm fine, thanks," implying things are not fine at all!

There are many popular books on nonverbal communication, present language that can be learned, the implication meaning of nodding, eye movement, and gesture is real feelings and intentions a person is understood.

Write down wrong gestures.

Communication Skill

Beginning with being a good listener, this is the first key is to listening. Communicate at your best by using verbal talk. When communicating with someone, try to not interrupt. Try not to put your two cents, not talking while the other person is talking. Give time to listen. An active listener pays close attention to the talker. When the person who is talking finishes, then you may speak.

One habit that I used to be bad at was to truly listen when people spoke. I zoned out. I was distracted or my attention started wandering before they stopped talking.

Begin a good listener is:

- Communication.
- Tips of best communication.
- Job.
- Eye contact

Active listeners pay close attention to what other people are saying, questions to clarify and to ensure understanding.

In active listening, you will have a better understanding of what the other person is saying so you can respond approximately.

Make a list of inappropriate speaking.

I Just Love that Man

Let's take a look at yourself. In order for someone to love you, you have to first love yourself.

Before you take on this relationship called love, "love you." No one can love you the way you should love yourself.

Come into a relation with someone first to see if they love themselves first.

Here are some tips:

1. How do they talk?
2. Do they say, "I love me some me?"
3. Repetition is the key.

We put on a mask before leaving the house. We make it seem that we have it going on. I don't think so. Be real with yourself. We will learn that coping with life is not easy but telling the truth in life is much easier. Lying makes it difficult to live. Why? Because you are a liar. Can I be real?

Make a list of self-improvements you need.

After this list is done, you will see the true you.

Self-Esteem

A lot of people say, "I'm real;" "I speak the truth;" "I just tell it like it is." Really? Wow.

Self-esteem is a term that is described as a person's own measurement of self-worth. How do you think about yourself?

A. Set of firmly placed values and principles.
B. Being able to trust your own judgment and not feeling guilty about choices you make.
C. Stop living in the past. Live fully in the present.
D. Believing in yourself.
E. Participating in outside activities.

I feel that when you are ready to go out and do you, first make sure you are ready for this world.

> This God, his way is perfect; the word of the LORD proves true; he is a shield for all those who take refuge in him. (Psalm 18:30)

Low self-esteem often comes in early childhood or as a child goes through teenage years. In early childhood, the attitude of parents projected toward a child impacts high or low esteem. When the parent ignores a child, low self-esteem will develop. When in school, low self-esteem may result from traumatic issues or from noninterest from peers and other adults.

I tell people that early childhood is the cause of low-esteem of adolescence. In the early stages of childhood, most of the time, low-esteem is from what the child sees or hears. Sometimes there is name-calling from the parent or abuse.

Write down when your trauma started for you.

I Wear a Title

I have seen many people say horrible things to people in leadership (that makes you better than them).

1. Having a poor understanding of people.
2. Having personal issues within self.
3. Very disorganized.

Envisioning a better life, setting goals, and following through with goals I feel you can impact first requires leading yourself. Often, leadership has to be learned. Keeping ourselves inspired, motivated, we need to lead ourselves with our hearts and have a purpose and devotion.

God desires those who are called out of the world to be His chosen ones. What does it mean to be called and chosen? This means that you are called by God to serve people with all your heart; not with your heart but God's heart. It's important to understand one's calling is from God! Only He calls you. "No one can come to me unless the Father who sent me draws him" (John 6:44).

But we are here to give thanks to God always for you. We are loved by the Lord because from the beginning, you were chosen by the true and living God (Amen) through sanctification by the Spirit of God to which He called you by the Gospel.

> Such teachings come through hypocritical liars whose consciences have been seared as with a hot iron. (1 Timothy 4:2)

I'm Just Playing

Remember when he or she said, "Girl, you are fat." Yes? How did you feel? The answer is you felt hurt. Insulting names is emotional and is mental abuse. In this situation, we look at how this relates to you. The one that's doing name-calling is a person that was hurt in the past. Do you agree? Honesty is the best way to communicate. This is how you do this: "Johnny, I felt hurt when you said I am fat."

Johnny says, "Girl, I was just playing. I won't say it again."

The Bible says, "Praise you because I am fearfully and wonderfully made; your works are wonderful, I know that full well" (Psalm 29:14).

Let's pray for strength that God will make you strong in all areas of your life to where no one will say something to you and you are hurt.

Father, in the name of Jesus, now I come asking you to make me strong. God, I need your strength, your power to make me strong and to build me up in you, Jesus.

Make a list of your hurts.

Expectations

Definition of expectation: A strong belief that something will happen or be the case in the future.

Expectation is where you are expecting someone to do. Don't assume something; don't look for it to happen.

All disappointment, resentment, and wanting it to happen can, over time, that combination this is the problem waiting other. You step up and stop waiting and expect others to meet your needs. Domineering will not fulfill expectations that go on: I do everything I should.

Except who you are, stop thinking someone owes you because they don't.

Habit with shortcomings:

1. Comparisons are always unfair. Stop comparing the worst we know of ourselves to the best like others.
2. Comparisons, but only a person who believes every good thing can be counted (or measured). Don't be played.
3. Comparisons rob us of space and time. We all get 86,400 seconds each day. Even one to compare yourself or your accomplishments to another person is one moment too many.
4. You are too unique. Your gifts and talents and successes will make you very successful if used correctly.

Write no expectations.

> Each one should use whatever gift he has received
> to serve others, faithfully administering God's
> grace in its various forms. (1 Peter 4:10 NIV)

Your Other Self

Merging into one's self, controlling your other self, when you were a little boy or girl, something happened to you. Think back. The reason I have you to do this is because something in you needs to be expose.

This is why it is very important to have God in your life so you can pray to the Father in heaven. He answers all prayers. God loves you. He's caring and understanding.

Take a look at your life today. Are you happy? Are you now where you want to be in life?

Answer these questions.

After these questions are answered, be sure you tell the truth.

The truth will set you free!

The Bible says: "And you will know the truth, and the truth will set you free."

Let's pray. Father, in the name of Jesus, I pray that you will touch this person now and I pray that truth and understand will be revealed in the name of Jesus. I demand and declare that this person will be set free today.

Facing the Giant in Your Life

The giant seems so big, but guess what? It's not if you trust the true and only God for that situation. Job's loss, divorce, financial problems, abuse, addictions, physical and emotional pain, illness, cancer, and death are just a few problems. We face problems in our thoughts. Our own mind often takes us to *another level; it seems larger than it really is.*

Don't hesitate to face the problem.

David was not a soldier. He simply went to the battlefield to deliver food to his brothers as he was instructed by his father. Upon learning of the giant, David set himself up to fight this huge soldier that left grown men running in fear (1 Samuel 17:32). *Don't run from your problems. Face them head on without hesitation. Trust that if God brings you to it, He will also bring you through it.*

Be determined and strong.

For many, this is a very difficult time to pray. This is a very good time to pray. Ask for help. Your heavily Father hears your need. This is how you pray: You start by asking for forgiveness of your sin. Why? Because the Bible says God does not hear the prayer of the sinner.

If you declare with your mouth, "Jesus is Lord," and believe in your heart that God raised him from the dead, you will be saved (Romans 10:9).

Write down your giants.

Relationship Issues

Anger is learned. The person who is angry begins to teach the person that's not angry to begin to come out. Why? He or she fears for their life or safety. This begins when someone sees or experiences this kind of problem.

As we begin to learn anger, feeling, and emotions, your breakthrough is now.

Now you will learn why you are so angry.

1. Build-up
2. Arguing
3. Stuffing
4. Disappointment
5. Expectations

The anger is in you. It's now begun to surface (activate), making you feel lost, hurt, disappointed, hopeless, and sad.

Begin to write down how 1–5 makes you feel.

How Do You Feel After Writing?

Express in your writing.

Don't write past this line.

The reason is you will begin to write a book. It's not time. Just begin to reflect on how you felt when this issue began.

The Bible says in 1 Peter 4:13, "Instead, be very glad—for these trials make you partners with Christ in his suffering, so that you will have the wonderful joy of seeing his glory when it is revealed to all the world."

Your behavior is learned. We see and hear by experiences we suffer through this relationship called love. This is really true love.

I pray in the mighty name of Jesus that God will touch you in a way where right now, you feel His power as you begin to feel the anointing on your life. I know God can heal your issues right now. Amen.

What Is My Need, Want, and Desire?

Let's begin to look at your relationship now, as in begin to feel, blame, point the finger.

Let's begin as a child go as far back that you can remember. Dad and Mom—was there or not two parents? Or maybe one? Begin to see where you first saw a man or woman, which should have been your dad or mom. If not, then move forward. First let me say you didn't ask to be here, so don't get mad. Thank God that you are here. Don't lose your train of thought, It's not your fault. Forgive so you can move past your feelings.

This means there may have been no parents. It doesn't matter at this point (why) you are here. Rejoice.

How do you feel at this point?

Begin to write.

The Bible says in Matthew 6:14–15, "For if you forgive other people when they sin against you, your heavenly Father will also forgive you. But if you do not forgive others their sins, your Father will not forgive your sins."

Post-traumatic Stress Disorder (PTSD)

I myself have been in this very place that's not nice. I write about this because of my experience six months ago from two years before that no one knew.

People may think that this kind of illness comes from car wrecks, physical harm, etc. No, it is stress of life. Let's take a few moments and deal with the depression of your life. Where do we begin? You may have experienced a traumatic abuse, drugs, alcohol, rape, etc. Whatever happens, "you still live."

The Bible says, "But understand this, that in the last days there will come times of difficulty. For people will be lovers of self, lovers of money, proud, arrogant, abusive, disobedient to their parents, ungrateful, unholy, heartless, unappeasable, slanderous, without self-control, brutal, not loving good, treacherous, reckless, swollen with conceit, lovers of pleasure rather than lovers of God, having the appearance of godliness, but denying its power. Avoid such people… (2 Timothy 3:1–8).

Write down your hurts.

Admit to Wrong

Admit to the truth. Be real with yourself.

1.   Negative people have got to go.

Deal with other people's problems, especially when swamped in your own mess. What? But how much longer are you going to be their emotional fix? Will they ever learn to change? Save yourself from the drama! Be with positive people who can lift you up as you do for them.

2.   Express feelings and opinions.

Speak out, even if it might hurt others. Using the word *hurt* my sound harsh. Have you noticed that people who hurt people have the most problems? In the form of a critical remark to their ego or beliefs, say it anyway. Because people who can't be open or accept you for being you are insecure with their own selves. They just can't face reality without losing control of their emotions. If anything, the people you should surround yourself with are those who welcome your honest opinion and aren't afraid to get their ego bashed.

3.   Stand behind your words.

People take words very seriously. And if you tend to say things without believing in them, they'll start questioning your mindset and break it down until your weakness is fully exposed. If you want to get real with yourself, secure your values and beliefs, and have a legitimate answer to what you think feels right. Words make up your authenticity. So say what you mean and mean what you say.

4. Take advice you have evaluated carefully.

Just because it is right for them doesn't mean it is right for you. Most of us carry this conception that there's one solution for everything, be it high-end skincare products for the flawless skin, LinkedIn for job opportunities, college for a six-digit salary, etc. But the truth is there's more than one thing that works. And the only way you would know is by taking every piece of advice with a grain of salt and evaluating.

Conflicts to Avoid

In the moment of a heated situation, it's easy to say something you'll regret. If we learn to collect our thoughts before saying ugly words, is it really easy to get the person to understand what not to say?

1. Express your anger.

Take a few moments to think clearly about frustration in an assertive but in a nonconfrontational way. Say what you mean in a nice way without hurting others or trying to control them.

2. Exercise

Physical exercise can help bring stress levels down. If you feel your anger escalating, go for a fast walk or run or sometimes, do your physical activities.

3. Take a break.

Timeouts aren't just for kids. Take short breaks during the day so you will feel better, less stressed. A few moments of quiet time might help you feel better doing the day so that you may not feel irritated or angry.

4. Identify positive solutions.

Instead of focusing the negative, take back your control. Work on self-improvement. You can learn how to take back full control of your life. Choose to be great at what you are and accept who you are. God has created you to be great. Choose life, not death, meaning you will identify with the issue and solve this problem by learning to love yourself first.

How to Recover from Your Past

Recognize that this pain is not forever. To get over something you have to go through, there is a process, a healing you have to get over. This is why we have to know that there are people that can heal you from all hurt and pain.

The Bible says in Psalm 91:9–10, 14–16: "Because thou hast made the Lord, which is my refuge, even the Most High, thy habitation; there shall no evil befall thee, neither shall any plague come nigh thy dwelling. Because he hath set his love upon me, therefore will I deliver him: I will set him on high, because he hath known my name. He shall call upon me, and I will answer him: I will be with him in trouble; I will deliver him, and honor him. With long life will I satisfy him, and show him my salvation."

How do you heal emotional pain?

Healing emotional stress and pain.

1. Be real; tell the truth.
2. Turn to positive speaking.
3. Avoid negative people.
4. Speak life into you.

In your pain and healing, let go of people that are negative.

1. Cut off the past.
2. Forgive yourself.
3. Forgive others who hurt you.
4. Love yourself.

How Do You Feel?

I think you did very well. Sometimes we hold in what we want to say when we are children and have no voice. This is how you get rid of anger. Write it down, and throw it away. Is it so unfair to be blamed for something you did not do? Wow, this is a way to show I am the bigger person. I won because I stayed quiet and honored my parents or elders (I am so pride of you).

Jesus honored his mother and father.

1) Pray for your father and mother.
2) Keep on helping them, even though it's difficult at times.
3) Model Jesus for them.
4) Exercise strength in front of them.
5) Cry for them to the Lord; pour your heart out to God on their behalf.
6) Please forgive them. The Lord will help you do this!

Trust me, all is well! God has your back.

Let's pray. Father, in the name of Jesus, I pray for my parents/ the absent parents in my life and that You will be my shelter when I'm lonely. I pray that You will be a help in my time of need.

I want you to pray now!

Failure from Fear

How can you not to be afraid of failure?

Think of a situation in which you are afraid of failure. Visualize yourself now hitting an obstacle, allow yourself to feel the fear, and then see yourself moving forward. Next, spend a few minutes planning *how to overcome* whatever obstacles may stand in your way. Then see yourself succeeding despite these obstacles.

Read more about it or talk to a mental *health* professional.

1. Failing makes you worry about what other people think about you.
2. Failing makes you worry about your ability to pursue the future you desire.
3. Failing makes you worry that people will lose interest in you.
4. Failing makes you worry about how smart or capable you are.
5. Failing makes you worry about disappointing people whose opinion you value.
6. You tend to tell people beforehand that you don't expect to succeed in order to lower their expectations.
7. Once you fail at something, you have trouble imagining what you could have done differently to succeed.

About the Author

Kathleen Hall is a self-made businesswoman, mother of three adult children, foster parent to a one-year-old little boy, and a cancer survivor. She is an entrepreneur in the field of cosmetology and in the selling of major beauty, hair, and jewelry products. Styling hair is her passion, and she has been providing her services to the community for thirty-nine years.

She is an inspiration to many people in her line of work, but most of all, to all the women in her life. She is a cancer survivor who, through her faith, was able to overcome and has been in remission for almost three years. Her drive and determination to continue on her path to live her best life demonstrates her strength in continuing to lead and to help men and women pursue their goals and dreams.

She attended seminary school in 2012 at the Spirit of Liberty Global Ministries under the leadership of Dr. Larry J. Lloyd, PhD, Founder/Dean. She also completed courses in Christian education, African American Systematic Theology, and the role of Men and Women in the Church Leadership.

Kathleen Hall is a beacon of hard work, determination, and dedication to everything she sets her mind to. It's been a great honor having her in my life.

Marisol Lopez

Sister in Faith, Friend, Businesswoman, Wife, and Mother of Four Daughters.